Today Pauline and the girls are going to play games with their Playtime Truck. It has lots of special features.

Lots of space inside for toys

Playhouse

Loud speaker connected to a musical hooter

Extra-wide seat

Roll-up slides

Drop-down doors

D1394997

Slidetime

Pauline and the girls have set up the slides on the **Playtime Truck** and their friends have got their tickets ready for slidetime.

Songtime

Now Pauline has pressed the musical hooter
and is driving up
the hill.

"Come on, girls, let's sing."

"The Grand Old Duke of York,
He had ten thousand men.
He marched them up to the top of the hill,
And he marched them down again.
And when they were up, they were up,
And when they were down, they were down,
And when they were only halfway up,
They were neither up nor down."

Bash and Bounce

The girls love it when they play
Bash and Bounce with their mum.

"Hold tight, girls!"

Giorgio is zooming down the hill in his
Little Ball Car.

Beep! Beep!

"Here I come!"

A Fruit Break

Pauline and the girls have set up the Playtime Café.

"I love bananas."

"I love apples."

Play-time Café open

They have invited Stacie, Jo-Jo and Clemence to join them for a fruit break.

The Big Play

Pauline and the girls have asked Mr Thornton-Jones and friends to help unpack the toys from the Playtime Truck.

"What time is it? It's..."

"Playtime!"
"Hiss!"
"This is fun!"
"Brmm! Brmm!"
"Oops! my glasses!"
"Look at me!"
"Whee!"

Bye-bye, Pauline and the girls

Pauline and the girls have had great fun with their Playtime Truck. Pauline has pressed the musical hooter to play a gentle lullaby and here is everyone having a good sleep.